DEATH by BURNOUT

Education's Dirty Little Secret

Dr. SHERIKA SIMONE

Death by Burnout:
Education's Dirty Little Secret

Published by Sherika Simone

Copyright © 2020 by Sherika Simone
All rights reserved.
Book Cover Design by Erika T. Neal
Illustration by Fitzroy Dacres
Editor: Shana Lark
For more information, contact:
Dr. Sherika Simone
Email: Sherika.Simone7@gmail.com
FB: facebook.com/drsherikasimone
IG: Instagram.com/drsherikasimone

ISBN: 9781075711862

For dad.

BURNOUT: Prolonged exposure to ongoing stressors in the work environment leading to increased emotional exhaustion, detachment from the job, and decreased feelings of personal accomplishment.

-Christine Maslach

CONTENTS

	Acknowledgments	i
	Preface	iii
1	I COULDN'T SAVE HIM … BUT I HAD TO SAVE MYSELF	1
2	FIGHTING THE BATTLE, BUT LOSING THE WAR	27
3	LOCKED AWAY	53
4	HOLD ON… THIS TOO SHALL PASS	75
5	BAD APPLES	97
6	I WILL KILL YOUR BABY!	117
7	DON'T CHANGE HORSES MIDSTREAM …OR SHOULD YOU?	137
8	WEATHERING THE BURN	165
	Epilogue	187
	Glossary	191
	References and Further Readings	193

ACKNOWLEDGEMENTS

First, I give thanks to God for giving me a heart of compassion and a desire for helping others.

I also express my sincere gratitude to all the teachers nationally who have participated in sharing their experiences with being burned out. Thanks for sharing your truth.

To my family and friends, thanks for your continuous motivation, ongoing support, and unwavering belief in me.

PREFACE

The unspoken truth about teacher burnout is that it's never really talked about. It's that little secret that some may have heard about, most experience, and almost everyone turns a blind eye to. But why is burnout among teachers not being discussed more on a wider platform among stakeholders such as district and school leaders and teachers who are directly impacted by it and with those who have the power to impact change?

Think for a moment, when was the last time you had a discussion among your peers about being burned out? Furthermore, when was the last time you attended a faculty meeting where you talk about your experiences of being burned out? Reflect on all the year(s) you have been in this profession, when have you ever attended a professional development where you discussed the symptoms of burnout, strategies to decrease burnout or coping with being burned out?

Teacher burnout has been a topic of conversation for decades and has continued to pique the interest of researchers. In 2019, The World Health Organization (WHO) officially recognized burnout as a syndrome, which can be diagnosed by clinicians. The International Classification of Diseases (ICD)-11 has also updated their definition of burnout to reflect Maslach's (1982) widely acceptable definition: feelings of increased emotional exhaustion, increased withdrawal from work, and reduced feelings of professional efficacy. The concept of burnout first came about in the 1970s coined by an American psychologist named Herbert

Freudenberger. Since then, dozens of researchers and hundreds of articles and books have been written addressing the issue of burnout among individuals in the helping profession (e.g., teachers, lawyers, doctors, police officers, and therapist).

My journey to the realization of the existence of burnout came about one afternoon as I sat in my classroom preparing for my next days of lessons. After all of my colleagues had left, when the boisterous noise in the school had halted, and the sound of the crisp wind whistled through the building, I began to question myself. "What am I still doing here? Why can't I seem to tear myself away from all the work I have to do? Why do I feel that nothing I am doing is making a difference?" Interestingly, this was not the first time I had stayed until 6pm. Sometimes I had even stayed until 8pm, working late. Surely, this could not be healthy. Like me, hundreds of other teachers have given up spending valuable time with family and friends, and have sacrificed time to rest and relax to remain at work to get caught up with their lesson plans, grade papers, prepare for an observation, or just to collaborate with colleagues. But the cost they will later pay for such commitment may be deadly.

They say knowledge is power. After realizing that I had become burnout's next victim, I sought to understand more about this phenomenon. This quest for enlightenment led me on an extensive search. The literature surrounding teacher burnout was ample. Teachers were suffering and they were suffering doing what, for most, was a lifelong dream. A dream that they believed they were born to fulfill. This new found awareness about teacher burnout has led me to tap into the lived experiences of teachers who have succumbed to this plight, those who continue to battle with it, and those who have thrown in the towel and said enough is enough.

This book takes you into the lives of several teachers across the United States who have experienced burnout in some facet. Their names, other identifiable information, and some events were changed to protect their privacy and for confidentiality. Their stories give us a bird's-eye view into the heart of their struggle and detailed accounts of factors that contributed to them becoming burned out. Each of their stories conclude with offerings of suggestions on how to hopefully decrease the impact of teacher burnout.

Before you begin this journey into their experiences, I would like to leave you with this statement shared with me by one of the teachers.

"It is not ok to just sit by the wayside and ponder the 'what ifs.'
It is not ok to just turn a blind eye to the issues that so easily and frequently beset us.
It is not ok to say, someone else can fix 'it' versus taking a stand to help fix 'it.'
But what is ok is that we rally *together* for the greater good. To join shoulder to shoulder, with one determination to decrease the impact of teacher burnout."

-Jane

01

I COULDN'T SAVE HIM ... BUT I HAD TO SAVE MYSELF

"There is nothing more damaging to a person's self-efficacy than the lack of *self-efficacy* itself."

"**W**hat the hell just happened?!"

"This can't be happening. Not again, not again, not again!" Mr. Allen muttered.

Mr. Allen froze in his tracks. For about 10 seconds, it seemed like time stopped, then replayed in slow motion.

Unsure what to do, Mr. Allen yelled, "Melvin – Melvin. Hey, Hey man! Stop… just stop!"

As a first year teacher, Mr. Allen wanted a change. In his previous career, he was displeased with his job. Things were mundane, unsatisfactory, just not what he had hoped for. He wanted to make a difference, to change someone's life, and what he was doing was just not it.

Mr. Allen graduated from a local university in his hometown.

"This was a big accomplishment," he recounted as he discussed his journey, which has now led to him becoming an educator.
As a first generation college graduate, he knew how important completing college would be.
He recalled the struggles that he endured while in college: not much family support, or any family members who had gone through a similar experience to share with him.

"It was costly, I won't lie, but my family rallied around me and they all put together to help me pay for college," he said proudly.

On the day he graduated, more than 2 dozen family members showed up at the graduation ceremony. Although only 9 were able to get inside the ceremony hall, Mr. Allen said, "They were all excited and proud to experience this moment. It was like they all graduated with me. This degree was for all of us."

It did take a while for Mr. Allen to find his way to the classroom. After graduating, his first priority was to start making money. But he later saw that making money was not as fulfilling as he hoped.

After several years in the corporate world, Mr. Allen decide to leap into the field of education. And this he recalled was a move he thought was well worth it.

Teacher shortage is and continues to be a recurring quandary in the education system. As quickly as teachers enter, they leave. Some do stay for a while, several years at best, but soon leave.

———————

"I knew as soon as I wrapped up my interview that I was ready. I was definitely ready and this was the right fit for me." Mr. Allen recalled.

But within the first 3 months of his first year as a teacher, things were *not* what he had expected.

Mr. Allen said he was told repeatedly that as a first year teacher, it is good to get to know your students, to understand their background, to make them like you and they will comply.

"But when you are faced with a disruptive student that becomes a tough battle. When I came face to face with a disruptive student, I felt I had only three options:
- Call the front office
- Redirect the student

- Ignore the behavior

On this day, I chose option one," Mr. Allen said.

Mr. Allen darted for the phone and dialed 222, for the front office.

"Please, can you have one of the deans come to room 118? I need someone now! Melvin is at it again," Mr. Allen said.

"… Oh no," Mr. Allen thought to himself after hanging up the phone. "I probably shouldn't have done that? Maybe this time I should have just ignored him."

Last week Mr. Allen met with his mentor for their weekly meeting. He was tossing around in his head how to deal with Melvin. Mr. Allen blamed himself for what he was going through.

"Clearly I had a problem. It was me, it had to be me," Mr. Allen thought.

Mr. Allen just could not fathom how this could be happening and of all times, NOW!

"It was too early in the school year to be dealing with this. What else can I do to help decrease his defiant and disruptive behaviors in class?" Mr. Allen thought.

Mr. Allen started slowly. "So I have this kid in my class" Mr. Allen began as he finally built up the courage to voice his frustration to his mentor about Melvin.

"I have this boy in one of my classes, he just keeps messing around. He is disruptive, defiant, intimidating at times, and sometimes he even gets physical by pushing the desk or the chair over. He is such a pain. *I can't teach*," Mr. Allen stated with a deep sigh of despair. "I don't know what else to do."

The research does not lie. Teachers are on the frontline when it comes to facing the horrors of students' disruptive and violent behaviors. Violence towards teachers and peers has taken over classrooms across the nation, and by the looks of it, it's not getting better.

With a quick search on the World Wide Web using search terms 'teacher attacked by student' or 'teacher student fight' reveals a myriad of videos, blogs, news stories, and articles documenting this growing and disturbing trend.

"A child kicked me so hard that I needed to have knee reconstruction surgery."
Teacher report, CEA.org, 2018

"My colleague was in her second trimester of pregnancy" {when she was assaulted}.
Teacher report, CEA.org, 2018

"I have been violently shoved around my classroom."
Teacher report, CEA.org, 2018

And the list goes on and on and on. In 2018, Jackson Lucas wrote an article titled, "Violence against Teachers is a National Crisis." In his article he discussed the limited research into violence against teachers. He pointed out that while some violence incidents are being reported others are not, thus leading to contradiction in statistical reports regarding violence against teachers. He noted that teacher victimization is increasing. 80% of teachers stated that they were the target of one or more violent encounter from students within a 12 month period. As if that report is not enough:

94% of teachers experienced violent behaviors toward them. Teachers reported being victimized by students.
-Lucas, 2018

Almost 73% of teachers experienced verbal threats, intimidation, and obscene gestures.
-Lucus, 2018

> ***More than 40% of teachers were physically attacked.***
> ***-Lucas, 2018***

Violence against teachers in not a new issue, but this violence has become a national crisis.

Melvin was a seventh grader who had made a name for himself within the first nine weeks of sixth grade. Most of the faculty and staff knew of him. His behavior had become out of control. Precautionary methods were implemented prior to confronting him. He was quite unpredictable. Oftentimes administrators and teachers bargained with him to diffuse situations or to prevent embarrassing situations from happening. Other times they bribed him, promising him time out of class with them, running errands for them, or bringing in a favorite item of his.

Melvin was running the show… literally, and he knew it.

"Ok - ok, I got this. A dean will be here shortly, I just need to talk him off the cliff" Mr. Allen thought to himself.

"But something went off in Melvin's head. He - He - snapped, he just went *crazy*!"

"He flipped over the desk he was sitting at, went over to the desk of another student and flipped that desk, sending it in my direction. I froze."

Mr. Allen expressed how alarmed he was having not seen Melvin at this level before. "He was like a beast! It was like I was outside of my body watching all this unfold. I couldn't move, I just couldn't… Nothing prepared me for this."

> *According to research, student disruptive behavior is one of the leading contributor of teachers' expressed feelings of emotional exhaustion, leading to burnout.*
> -Aldrup, Klusmann, Ludtke, Gollner, Trautwein, 2018

But what has been done so far to help remedy this issue?
In addition to encouraging teachers to report these incidents, dedicating resources to examining the root cause of such violence, educating teachers of types of attacks, safety strategies, and teacher support, can and in time, work toward eradicating this problem.

"Everything stood still at that moment," Mr. Allen continued as he recalled the event step by step.

"Instruction stopped. In that time there was nothing I could do."

The students' eyes were glued on him, as if playing a game of chess and waiting for the next move.

Mr. Allen slowly backed away from the flipped desk. "Melvin stood still, with his fist clenched, his breathing restless and loud, he steered at me with piercing eyes."

Mr. Allen repeated over and over in his head, "They are coming, someone has to be coming," as he stood motionless behind the desk.

"I waited, and waited, and waited for

what appeared to be an eternity. But, no one showed up. No one showed up!"

The bell rang and Melvin darted for the door. "He stopped, cracked opened the door and turned around slowly. The glare of the light from outside gave him a silhouette representing an angel, only he was not, not today."

"F*** you, Mr. Allen," he shouted.

Students chuckled as they scurried past Melvin to leave.

"Owwwww," one student responded.

"You're gonna get a referral!" another uttered.

"Whatever," Melvin replied.

"F*** you, motherf***er," he yelled again as he pointed his middle finger in my direction.

"Melvin stared at me. He looked me up and down, as if to challenge me. He waited for about three seconds, standing motionless, fearless as if he was waiting for me to say something. To do something. But I didn't… I couldn't."

Melvin left the room.

"What the hell just happened?
"What the hell just happened?
"I - I had to sit down. This did not just happen.
"I sat for maybe about 10… maybe 15 minutes. I still couldn't process what just happened.

"I barely recalled what happened in the other classes following Melvin's class. I tried to continue with the lessons, but I was just in a daze."

After work Mr. Allen shared with his colleagues and mentor what had transpired in his class earlier that day with Melvin.

"What?"

"Really?"

"No way?!" They responded simultaneously as Mr. Allen shared detail by detail about Melvin's classroom incident.

"But there is so much more, it's not just today, it's not just Melvin. His action today is just the icing on the cake.

"I am fed UP!"

There is a profound cost to teachers being victimized. Like Mr. Allen, teachers across the nation are fed up. Additionally, teachers are experiencing feelings of anxiety, depression, lacking engagement among peers and students. They are being impacted emotionally, physically, and spiritually.

Melvin's disruptive behaviors and defiance didn't stopped there. They escalated. Week after week, multiple phone calls home, attempts for parent-teacher conferences, referrals after referrals, suspensions after suspensions. But nothing changed. Melvin continued to attend class as usual, except when he was suspended or absent. He didn't complete his work and any attempt Mr. Allen made to engage in a respectful conversation with him was a lost cause.

"I couldn't save him… but I had to save myself."

As educators we believe that we have the ability to change lives, to make a positive impact in the lives of those we teach. Grounded at the base of our hearts are our nurturing tendencies. We are caretakers, role models, providers, leaders.

At times we are our students' only hope, only push to achieve a better education, a better future. But the reality of life is that there are factors in this profession that hinders us from fully carrying out our mission, from fully impacting in a positive way, the students we are fortunate to educate. So what do we do?

According to the theory of social learning, Self-efficacy is an individual's belief in his or her ability to achieve one's goal or how well he or she is able to execute a task. Unless a person perceive that his or her action will bring about change, such a person will be less proactive to undertake a task in the face of adversity.

-Bandura, 2010

But can we really make a change?
Is it worth it?
And at what cost?

"Violence against teachers and the consequences that follow, negatively impact teacher recruitment and retention by discouraging potential educators from entering the field of education. Lack of knowledge on teacher victimization has left many schools unable to provide the support network necessary for the teacher, and ultimately student, success."
-Lucas, 2018

Mr. Allen made a decision, a decision to make a change, to save himself. This was more important than struggling with the negative impact of student behaviors.

"No one will take care of you if you don't take care of yourself.
"No one will take care of you if you don't take care of yourself," Mr. Allen recited over and over.

His lifeless stare was like looking into the heart of a vaporized soul.

"I didn't think they would break me.
 "But - But, they did."

> *More than 40% of new teachers quit teaching within the first five years, with up to 50% of teachers leaving within five years.*
> *- National Education Association, 2018*

Mr. Allen was a first year teacher who

did not overcome the plight of the classroom to make it into a second year.

Teachers are not lining up to be burned out. They are not fervently waiting to be violated physically. They are not waiting for superman to appear and save them from the *woes* that plague our educational system.

But for the few that still remains, the few that still hold fast that they can indeed make a change.

"Hold fast," they say.
"Stand strong."
"A change is coming."

So, where do we go from here?
What solutions can be offered to help ease teachers' experiences of burnout caused by students' negative behaviors?

Well, there is no one size fits all strategy when dealing with students' negative behaviors. But some examples that teachers have professed will help decrease the occurrence of students' negative behaviors are:
- Positive teacher-student relationship
- Teacher's cultural awareness
- Increased positive verbal praise
- Clear and concise expectations
- Seeing through the eyes of your students

"Sometimes what we call 'failure' is really just necessary struggle called *learning*.

Believe in yourself and all that you are.
Know that there is something inside you that is greater than any obstacle."

– Christian D. Larson

02

FIGHTING THE BATTLE, BUT LOSING THE WAR

"A CRUST EATEN IN PEACE IS BETTER THAN A BANQUET PARTAKEN IN **ANXIETY**."

—Aesop

"This morning, I sat through my entire professional learning committee meeting (PLC) wondering what the f*** was I doing here?"

The thought of all the work Jennifer had to do, made her anxious, jittery, and uneasy.

"My mind is going non-stop, it's like a ruptured volcano in my head.

"I can't get a break! I just can never get a flipping break." Jennifer shouted to herself.

"I need to prepare for my first period class.
"Then I have to update my common board.
"Plus I have to print the worksheets before the bell rings.
"I need to make sure everything is in order for my observation later today."

Jennifer explained that others will ask or wonder, "Why didn't you do that the day before?"

"I would!" Jennifer shouted. "But like so many others, there is always a meeting to attend, paperwork to fill out, students' work to grade. It just never ends."

One by one the list of all the things Jennifer needed to do before class started began to unravel in her mind. The more she looked at the clock, the more her heart raced.

Jennifer recalled how horrible she felt. Her stomach was in knots. Her palms were sweating. Her forehead felt hot. Her head got light. She began to zone out. She was having a panic attack.

"What the f*** am I doing here?" Jennifer muttered under her breath.

"Are you ok?" one of her teammates asked.

"I'm fine. I'm just doing fantastic," she replied with a sarcastic chuckle.

"I'm just a bit nervous because I have so much to do," she continued.

"I'm overwhelmed.

"I'm frustrated.

"It's too much, too much to do and I have no time."

Jennifer caught herself shaking. She couldn't help it; she just began to cry, not just a puny, modest cry, she was bawling.

Before Jennifer could say another word, her teammate Silvia leaped over and pulled Jennifer into her arms.

"Girl, just go with the flow. Fake it till you make it. That's what I'm doing. That's how I have been able to cope," her teammate whispered as she consoled Jennifer.

> *Up to 50% of teachers leave teaching within the first 3 to 5 years because of the enormous amount of work they have to endure.*
> —Ingersoll & Perda, 2012

Up to 40% of teachers are predicted to leave the profession by 2024.
—Hinds, 2019

Yesterday, Jennifer stayed back in her classroom until 7:30pm preparing for her upcoming observation and working on her lesson plans for the following week.

The night before, she stayed up until the wee hours in the morning grading her students' most recent writing prompts.

"The stack of papers piled high in front of me seemed like a mountain that I would not be able to climb over."

When Jennifer eventually glanced at the time, it was 2 a.m. and the pile in front of her seemed like it never budged. However, Jennifer was adamant about getting all the papers graded.

"I had to get these papers completed before my PLC meeting in the morning."

Every Tuesday morning Jennifer and her subject area team met to review students' data based on weekly formative assessments or to discuss lesson plans. This week it was writing.

Her team had been teaching the fundamentals of writing and they completed a recent assessment to analyze students' comprehension and mastery.

"I knew that if I showed up without my data that would be one more thing to make me look unprepared," she uttered.

With groggy eyes, a mild headache, and mentally drained, Jennifer toiled through the night into the morning to complete grading the papers. She completed the work just before daylight.

According to research, on average teachers spend up to 5 hours per day; 25 hours per week outside of their normal working hours completing school related tasks. A significant number of the work before school, after school and on the weekends includes grading papers, reviewing and revising lesson plans.
-Murray, 2019; **NEA, 2018**

"I feel like my life is not mine anymore.

"I don't even feel like I am a teacher. It's all about paperwork, lesson plans, and data.

"Data this, Data that, but when do I teach? When do I really teach? It's no longer about my students."

Jennifer recalled that within the past 2 weeks on 4 separate occasions she spent time doing non-teaching tasks. One week she had to spend one of her planning periods completing input forms for her students. In another week she had spent a little over 2 hours attending an IEP (Individual Education Plan) meeting and attending a parent-teacher meeting.

"I was even asked - well told, to attend an IEP meeting during my planning time because they needed a regular education teacher at the meeting and I was the only one available during the time the parent could attend," Jennifer recalled.

> *More and more teachers are leaving the profession due to policies and practices -Strauss, 2019.*

Attending non-teaching related meetings and completing non-teaching tasks are factors contributing to symptoms of burnout. Teachers are becoming exhausted, overwhelmed, and drained. All the above, if experienced on a continuous basis, are indicators that a teacher is teetering on becoming burned out.

> *The overwhelming amount of workload experienced by teachers had led to teachers becoming emotionally exhausted, overwhelmed, and fatigued, all symptoms of*

burnout.
-Lawrence, Loi, & Gudex, 2019

"Sometimes there is almost absolutely no time to breathe. No time to do meaningful work that will benefit my students' academic growth."

Jennifer's experience is not new, nor is it unusual. Teachers across the state are voicing the same concern. The workload crisis has caused teachers from all walks of life with varied experiences in the field, new teachers and veteran teachers alike, to pack up and leave. This is just one of the negative effects of burnout.

"To top it off, I was asked last week to cover a fellow colleague's class 2 times because her substitute did not show up."

The amount of work a teacher is expected to, or required, to do can vary from school to school. The difference in how much one group of teachers are expected to do compared to another varies based on the principal and/or the area supervisor.

Jennifer recalled one year, about 3 months after the start of the new school year, her principal decided to implement a new method of data tracking.

"They summon us to an urgent and important before school meeting to discuss what they called an urgent matter concerning student's academic monitoring.

"Sounds intimidating, right? Well it was."

Jennifer recapped below how an abrupt change in procedure led to an immediate shift in her and her colleagues' workload and job expectations.

"The meeting started out with a harsh lashing of the tongue."

Jennifer said her and her colleagues were accused of not doing their job, not stepping up to the plate and not showing that they deserved to be a member of the team, the school.

"If you don't want to be here, just say it, I'll sign off on your paperwork today!" The principal remarked.

"The room was so silent you could hear a feather fall.

"No one moved, no one dared to ask a question.

"We all sat still and motionless."

Jennifer recounted how the principal rambled on and on and on. Detailing the steps that would be taken to ensure that teachers are abiding by what was required.

"The assistant principals will be meeting with each of you individually to see your data. And anyone who is not complying, I have told them to send me their names. I'll handle it.

"This is non-negotiable," the principal added.

"I was honestly frightened. You don't understand, these principals literally have your career, your livelihood in their hands. One negative referral, and you are blacklisted."

Approximately 25% of teachers reported experiencing some form of bullying during their teaching careers from students, principals or administrators.

—Long, 2014

"Well," The principal said while pacing back and forth in front of the team. "This is how it will work."

"Each teacher on each team will now analyze their individual data and both upload the information on a shared school document as well as print the data out and post it in a designated area of the classroom, visible to anyone who enters the room. The data should be categorized showing students failing, in between, and passing. "

Jennifer leaned over and whispered to her teammate at the table.

"We already do this."

They all shook their heads, "yes."

The principal continued, "I know the online system already has this information completed for you, but obviously you are all not using it, at least not effectively. The data should be transferred into a document that I will share with you to upload to a shared folder. Additionally, it should also be posted in your classrooms.

"That's it, have a good day," the principal mumbled.

"The tension and visible anger in the room could be cut with a knife," Jennifer recalled, "We were dismissed... just like that."

"Respect is the key determinant of high-performance leadership.

How much people respect you determined how well individuals perform."

-Brian Tracy

"The mood for the rest of the day blanketed the school like a dark cloud.

"I have no idea how we made it through that day."

At lunch Jennifer and some of her colleagues whispered with contempt and anger about the added work they will now need to complete.

"But we already do this, the computer generates the data, we as a group analyze the data, we plan how we will move forward. So why do they need this?"

"A waste of time," one teacher muttered

"I bet you, no one will be looking at the information," another said resentfully.

"One more thing added to my plate to do, as if I'm not already doing enough," Jennifer added.

"What I want to know is why, and what's the point of this."

The answer to those two questions were never thoroughly expressed by the principal or the assistant principals.

> ***The bible states: "Where there is no vision, the people perish."***
> ***- Proverbs 28:18 (KJV)***

Jennifer, her team, and the entire school quickly adjusted to the new process and procedure for data tracking.

They followed through like robots.

"We were being compliant. We did it because we were told we had to do it. That's just it."

By the 3rd month, Jennifer noted that teachers were just doing what they were commanded to do . . . just another "busy work."

"Someone somewhere figured they could just tack on something else on our plate to fulfil their job."

Since the implementation of the new data tracking system, the principal, assistant principal, and the coach had only communicated and followed up with them 3 times to talk about the data.

Before the end of the first half of the school year, Jennifer noted the meeting she attended.

"I'll never forget January 14th. It was our usually scheduled staff meeting.

"The entire staff gathered in the cafeteria after school. The leadership team congregated around us, then in walked the principal."

"Do you have it ready?" He motioned to the assistant principal.

"Yes," the assistant principal replied. Jennifer described what appeared to be the unveiling of a new data system.

"We have received a feedback from you all and it appears that the current data tracking process is not working efficiently as we expected. We are being a bit redundant," the principal stated.

"I know we are half way into the middle of the school year but we need to find a good system that works, one that we can adopt and stick to before the year ends. So we are going to move to a more seamless, less time consuming data tracking system. The coaches will share with you at your next department meeting."

"The news of this 'new system' couldn't have come at a worst time," Jennifer thought.

The state testing season was approaching. Teachers were in the middle of analyzing students' data to identify which standards should be focused on intently.

"A new data tracking system?! What the hell!" a colleague at Jennifer's table muttered.

Jennifer looked at the teammate next to her. She could see the defeat in her eyes. She knew that what happened next was inevitable.

Jennifer received a text early the next morning.

"Hey Jennifer, I won't be in today. Not feeling well."

The next two days, Jennifer's teammate did not show up to work. No call, no show.

After 3 days Jennifer received a message. Her teammate had decided to call it quits.

The message Jennifer received stated:

> I could not handle it anymore. It was getting so bad that I started to leave work with headaches. I would wake up in the middle of the night with cold sweats. I was

constantly thinking about all the things I had to do. I even started to have bowel issues. I was always anxious, always in a state of worry. I even had to talk myself into to getting out of the car every morning when I pulled into the school's parking lot. I went to see a psychiatrist because one day during one of my classes I thought I was having a mental breakdown. I just couldn't take it anymore.

Jennifer was experiencing some of the symptoms of being emotionally exhausted, one of the signs of being or becoming burned out.

> ***More than 58% of teachers have experienced some form of mental and***

physical health issues due to work related stress.

32% of teachers reported they get less than 6 hours of sleep per night.

58% of teachers are constantly tired due to high work demands.

-Anthony, 2019; Diaz, 2018

Like Jennifer's coworker, departure in the middle of the school year is a common occurrence among educators. More and more teachers are packing up and leaving. There is a visible cry for help. A call for action to decrease the impact of burnout among teachers.

So where do teachers go from here?

With every problem teachers face, there are some identifiable steps that can be implemented to remedy the issue. Some solutions that have been offered up to help alleviate becoming overwhelmed and burned out due to undue workload include:

- Know your limit, what you are able and not able to take on
- Ask for HELP
- Be assertive, learn to say "NO"
- Take time out to rehydrate
- Surround yourself with positive individuals

"What is important is seldom urgent, and what is urgent is seldom important."
-Dwight D. Eisenhower

03

LOCKED AWAY

"THERE CAN BE NO PROGRESS WITHOUT THE NECESSARY SUPPORT."

-Laura Perls

"Don't open the door!"

"Hahaha."

"Open the door man, that's not cool."

"Hahaha, this shit is funny."

Ms. Phillips went into the classroom closet just for a second to get some more art paper and in an instant things changed.

She never thought that her students would have played such a cruel trick on her.

Ms. Phillips has been an educator for 33 years. She grew up in a household where education was a constant. Her mother was also an educator, her siblings are also in education. So, for

Ms. Phillips becoming a teacher was following in her family's footstep.

"I saw my mother in her role as an educator and I admired that. I used to pretend to be a teacher when I was younger, and I guess it just became a part of me. It came natural. I fell right into place when I was in the classroom."

Ms. Phillips graduated with her bachelor's degree and shortly after decided to pursue her master's degree.

Upon completing her master's degree and internship, Ms. Phillips began as a substitute teacher.

"It was a slow start because I graduated during the middle of the school year," Ms. Phillips recalled.

As an Arts Education major, she did not immediately find a full-time teaching job upon graduating. However, her luck changed the following school year.

"I was hired as an Art teacher at an Elementary school located in a low socioeconomic school."

Ms. Phillips recalled how excited she was when she got the offer. "I remembered calling my mom to tell her the news. After all, I was following in her footsteps."

"Guys, this is not funny. You need to open the door right now!" Ms. Phillips yelled as she banged on the door.

Ms. Phillips became more and more furious as the seconds passed.

Four months ago, Ms. Phillips had a surgical operation. Not many of her colleagues knew.

She had just returned to work almost a month ago and was easing back into the routines and procedures of work.

"In some sense, I do blame teaching for me having to have this surgery. I also blame the children, it's just that it has gotten harder. Sometimes, I am just not up for it."

Ms. Phillips noted that not much changed. "The workload is still the same, I still take papers home to work on or grade every night, meetings every week. The same ole same.

"But the kids, oh man, they have gotten worse!"

Research shows that close to half of teachers across the nation are actively seeking an alternative career choice. This in part due to the negative impact of students' behavior on teachers.

58% of teachers blame the negative impact of their mental health on working in the classrooms.

-American Federation of Teachers, 2017 & Mahnken, 2017

Being bullied at work by students was cited as one factor leading to teachers' negative perception of their mental health.

Ms. Phillips has noticed a significant change in her students' behavior. They have become more disruptive, disrespectful, and defiant since the past school year and even since she has been out on recovery.

"Every day, it's like I'm banging my head against the wall, just trying to reach them, to get through to them so I can teach them something. But nothing works."

Ms. Phillips is a few years from retirement. Sure she could leave teaching now. She could quit tomorrow.

"But the thought of how much it would cost me alone for medical coverage for me and my husband, makes leaving the misery of teaching not an option, at least not before retirement."

She recalled a conversation she had with her husband after her surgery.

"You know, after my operation, I told my husband that I didn't want to go back to work. I was ready to be done with it. After all, I blamed work for me having to have this surgery. So much to do, the kids are horrible, I don't feel like my administrator believes in me or supports me. We crunched the numbers, weighed the pros and cons, but, it wouldn't work. So we decided

I'd just stick it out for 3 more years."

Classroom management is something Ms. Phillips is aware she needs help with. But she attest, "the students today were never like this 5 years ago!

"It's like every year, they get worse and worse."

Last year, Ms. Phillips was given the opportunity to attend a few classroom management trainings.

"Some of the strategies worked, but others, nope... they did nothing."

One of the first trainings she received, she was positive that it would make a difference. And it did.

"So they taught me how to strategically set up my classroom, so the frequently misbehaving students would not be close to each other."

She recalled how at first those students were defiant, they refused to move. She was able to enlist the help of the dean to make the classroom adjustment and it worked.

"This was one of the best changes I made and boy, it felt good. I was able to teach."

After being locked in the closet for what seemed like hours, the door swung open.

Principal Farrer, School Resource Officer (SRO) Trise, and Dean Sharpe all stood in the doorway.

"Thank you, Thank you!" I muttered.

"Are you ok?" Principal Farrer asked,

"I don't know," I replied.

"What's wrong with you kids, what's wrong with you?!" Ms. Phillips shouted.

"I couldn't help it, I just burst out crying.

"It was embarrassing, by far the most embarrassing experience I have ever had in my entire 33 years of teaching."

That afternoon, Ms. Phillips was rushed to the emergency room due to having stoke like symptoms.

The increased emotional stress from teaching has become an all-time high.

61% of teachers feel their jobs are stressful.

-Mahnken, 2017

58% of teachers say they have poor mental health due to working as a teacher.

More than 40% of the teachers surveyed reported being bullied. More than 3 times higher than employees in other work industry.

Around 50% of bullying comes from students to teachers.

- American Federation of Teachers, 2017

Being locked away in her classroom closet was not the first major behavior issue with students she has had this school year. Specifically with this class.

Ms. Phillips noted that she has repeatedly asked for help. Help with separating the students that were constantly causing trouble in this class. Help from administrators to drop in unannounced to see how the students were behaving.

"But no one helped.

"Write a referral," I was told.

"Assign a detention," another encouraged.

"Did you call the parent already?" they would ask.

"Yes, yes, and yes. I've done all that," I replied.

"What else do you want me to do? Nothing is working.

"Nothing was working."

Two weeks before the closet incident, there was a fight in Ms. Phillips' class.

"I called the front office to have one of the deans come to my classroom. I could sense that something was about to happen.

"You know, it's one of those gut feelings you have deep down. A feeling that you just cannot shake."

Ms. Phillips recalled, as soon as she hung up the phone, one kid got up, walked over to another and just started punching that kid. It was brutal.

"Stop! Stop!" I yelled.

"But they just kept going.

"Some of the kids moved away, some ran

outside the classroom.

"I quickly called the front office again and begged to have a dean come now. It's a fight for crying out loud!" I yelled.

The two students eventually stopped fighting.

"I waited, and waited, and waited.

"It took about 4 minutes before someone showed up!

"Can you believe that? Four whole minutes!

"Where was my help? Where were they?"

Administrators wield strong influence when it comes to teacher support. When teachers perceive they are not getting support from their administrators it can create a toxic work environment.

-Education Week, 2020.

After the closet fiasco, Ms. Phillips thought to herself, "How can there be progress when there is no support?

She met with her principal later that week. She recalled expressing to her administrator, the importance of making some changes in two of her classes.

"I need some support. Things are getting ugly in there."

Ms. Phillips proposed two options that she believed would help. But those were quickly dismissed and replaced with accusations of ineffective classroom management skills.

"I walked away from that meeting

feeling alone and defeated!"

Like other teachers who has faced repeated discipline issues with their students, Ms. Phillips had documented those students with whom she needed help.

"My many referrals showed that their behaviors are not getting better. I call home almost every day for a student in one of my classes. Sometimes three or four times for the same student."

"I will talk with him or her." The parent would say.

"I will assign him or her PASS [Positive Alternative to in School Suspension]," the dean would say.

"I can't just move a child from your class because he or she is acting up." The counselor would remark.

"Well, Ms. Phillips, I know that he or she is not a bad child. You just need to approach the situation a bit different to see what works best." My supervising administrator would comment.

Ms. Phillips wrote the referrals for the students who fought.

Five days later, with no follow up from her administrator or the dean, the students were back in her class . . . business as usual.

Lack of administrator support is deemed one of the most frequently reported reason for teachers leaving the profession completely or changing work locations.

-Sutcher, Darling-Hammond, & Carver-Thomas, 2006

"I continue to remind myself that all this will be over soon. Retirement is nearing. But, at what cost?

"At what cost will I continue to endure the mistreatments from the students who I yearn to teach?

"At what cost will I continue to be shunned and be denied support from my administrators? At what cost?"

Teachers are more than twice as likely to quit teaching when they perceive they do not have support from their administrators.

-Sutcher, Darling-Hammond, & Carver-Thomas, 2006

Ms. Phillips has not given up. She has not yet hung up her coat.

Her 33 years of being in the classroom did not leave Ms. Phillips without some bumps and bruises.

"They are a constant reminder of the sacrifices that I have paid for this career that I love so much." She stated.

So what's next?

Coupled with input from other classroom teachers, Ms. Phillips added some suggestions on how to survive working in an environment without the full support of your administrators.

- Remember why you chose this career
- Look at the glass half full
- Choose your battles
- Believe in yourself
- Stay strong and be encouraged

"I understood myself only after I destroyed myself. And only in the process of fixing *myself* did I know who I really was."
— Sade Andria Zabala

04

HOLD ON... THIS TOO SHALL PASS

"IT'S NOT THE **LOAD** THAT BREAKS YOU DOWN; IT'S THE WAY YOU CARRY IT"

-Lou Holtz

"They wanted to intimidate me, but I will not let them!"

Mr. Warren hastily made his way toward the back of the school in search of his classroom.

Already five weeks late for the start of the school year, Mr. Warren felt he was now behind the eight ball and this could determine his level of success with classroom management and having a successful school year.

"What are you looking at? Yo! Back up, you're in my space, daaaaamn?"

Mr. Warren paused for a second, then stepped backwards. In a nurturing and calm voice he responded,

"Kenny, I am just trying to see what you were working on. I am here to assist you with completing your missing work."

"I'm good, I don't need your help." Kenny remarked, as he waved Mr. Warren away.

"You see, in my past experience, when I started a school in the middle of the year, or even a few weeks after the start of the school year, I tend to have a lot more difficulty with classroom management. Students don't seem to want to give you the same level of respect as they would if you were there from the get go."

―――――――

Mr. Warren has been a teacher for 15 years.

"Education was not my first option. I'm a finance person, but when the market crashed in 2008, I had to make a change and the easiest was getting into education."

Mr. Warren pointed out that teaching sometimes has been a struggle for him.

"But I quickly lashed on."

"Growing up, I didn't come from a well off family. My family had to work hard."

Mr. Warren recalled that any chance he got to work and make money, he did. He pointed out that, when he got the opportunity to go to college, he majored in finance because he thought that would be the quickest way to make money. "I figured, I would graduate, get a job working making the big bucks."

"Things just came to a crouching halt when the market crashed. All the money I was making slowly deteriorated, the money I saved dwindled."

Bombarded with information from his new hire orientation, first week of school procedures, and bothered that he had missed the start of the school year, things were already starting to frustrate Mr. Warren.

As he rushed down the hallway, Mr. Warren became a bit misplaced.

"Excuse me. Do you know which direction is room 215?" Mr. Warren asked a colleague in the hallway.

"Yes," she responded. "Go straight ahead, take the stairway to the top floor, enter the double doors and room 215 will be in that hallway."

Mr. Warren proceeded hastily in the direction he was told.

Beeeeeeeeeeeeeeeeeeeep. The bell sounded just as he made his way to the back of the classroom to put his items down.

"But my board is not ready. Where is the attendance paper? I need to log into the computer. What can I do to start things off?" One by one these items sprung off in his head.

Knock, knock. Mr. Warren turned around and shot toward the door. "They are already here."

One after one they entered the classroom.

"Good morning.
"Welcome.
"Good morning.
"Welcome," he said to each student as they excitedly but voicelessly stroll by him.

"Hmm, I guess no one knows how to say good morning anymore," Mr. Warren thought to himself.

"Good morning," Mr. Warren nervously announced as he proceeded toward the front of the class.

"Good morning class," Mr. Warren added with a little more spunk and base in his voice.

A few students muffled back, "Good morning."
Scanning the classroom from side to side, Mr. Warren continued.

"My name is Mr. Warren and I am your 4th period teacher. I am excited to be here and I know this is going to be a great year!"

Mr. Warren recalled how unprepared he felt at that time.

"I was just not ready, nothing was ready."

He walked over to the board and carefully scribbled his name on it.

"Let's start with a little get to know you activity."

This activity was just what he needed to take the focus off him and to ease his first day jitters.

As a 15 year veteran, Mr. Warren has had experience teaching a diverse group of students. This year his focus was to support students who were identified early as having a year or two worth of academic gap.

But early on, he realized that along with working with his students to bridge their academic gap he was also responsible for tracking their academic progress, writing their IEPs as well as other students IEPs, serve as a resource person, and attend meetings. Achieving the above soon proved to be more difficult when coupled with students' negative behaviors.

> *"For God hath not given us the spirit of fear; but of power, and of love, and of a sound mind"*
> *-2 Timothy 1:7 (KJV)*

"Sometimes I sit at home, at school during my planning, or on my lunch break, and I wonder. Is this my calling? Is teaching really for me?"

Mr. Warren confessed that no matter what he does, no matter how much he tries to help, nothing works. Now he has begun to question himself.

Burnout is defined as increased emotional exhaustion, increased withdrawal from peers, and decreased

personal accomplishment (self-efficacy).
-Maslach and Jackson, 2001

Albert Bandura (1997) coined the term, self-efficacy. This is the belief a person has in his or her ability to execute a given task. One's ability to work to attain a goal.

It is very evident that Mr. Warren has started to question his ability to do his work.

Early on, Kenny had shown to be a very disrespectful and difficult student. But it was not just him. Actually, 95% of Mr. Warren's class was comprised of students with behavioral issues. Additionally, these students had an IEP or a 504 label.

Research indicates that teachers

working with students with special needs suffer greater teacher turnover compared to teachers working with other students.

"As a special education teacher, we have many hours of paper work to accomplish in addition to our teaching and planning. Time for this is not taken into consideration."
- American Federation of Teachers, 2017

12% of teachers who work with students with special needs switch to another school.

8% of teachers who leave are those working in special education compared to 6%.
-Fore, Martin, Bender, 2001

The second half of the school year had

begun. The workload that Mr. Warren had experienced thus far had been unremarkably excessive. While he would like to believe he was the outlier, it was only affecting him, he needed to find better management skills, he knew different. He was not the only one.

During the first nine weeks of school, Mr. Warren was bombarded with request to complete teacher input forms and attend IEP and 504 meetings. As expected of him, he did as requested, completed the forms and attended the meetings.

"Sometimes, I would have up to 3 inputs to complete each week. Plus, I would have to attend these meetings. It was a lot on top of what I needed to do." Mr. Warren recalled that as the second half of the school year approached, things took a turn for the worse.

"Things changed. I began to feel

overwhelmed."

The frequency and amount of teaching related task and non-teaching related tasks became excessive.

"It was as if I was working a part-time job," Mr. Warren recalled that he had never received any one on one training on how to effectively complete an IEP or 504. He was given a sample, and was told to ask a fellow colleague for help if needed.

Mr. Warren recounted one Wednesday afternoon as he was getting ready to leave work and the alert for his email inbox chimed.

"I should have known better than to open it. It was after 6. I needed to get out of here. But I opened the email."

Email:
Hello Mr. Warren, sorry for the short notice. I will need to move the meeting that was scheduled for next Friday to this Friday. I will need you to complete the IEP and collect the inputs from the teacher and have them ready for Friday.
Thanks…

"These are the things that affect me mentally. It's the end of the day Wednesday, and I will have just one day to write an IEP and collect teacher input for this meeting?"

Mr. Warren stated that last week in the middle of the weekend he received an email to say that he had an IEP to complete for a meeting the following Tuesday.

"I was going back and forth, should I start it, should I wait until Monday when I return to work. But, then I would leave work late and would have to work on it at home as well.

"The workload is a lot! It's overwhelming."

> *"This job is stressful, overwhelming and hard. I am overworked, underpaid, underappreciated, questioned and blamed for things that are out of my control."*
> *-American Federation of Teachers, 2017*

The symptoms and feelings that Mr. Warren mentioned above are typical of individuals who are experiencing burnout.

The problem that teachers are encountering along with the excessive workload, is the short notice and short turnaround time that they are expected to complete these tasks.

While Mr. Warren contributes his survival throughout the school year to the support and help of his teammates and a few immediate colleagues, he affirms that there is still too much to do.

"Work always comes home with me. When I go home, sometimes I just put my bag down, open the computer and pick up where I left off at school.

"My wife understands… at least I hope so."

More than 1/3 of teachers work for more than 16 hours at home on school tasks.

81% of teachers said they thought about leaving teaching due to the enormous amount of workload.

"I feel I have no life - I simply work and will very soon be one more statistic of a teacher who can't bear it any longer and will quit!"
-National Education Union, 2018

I began recording the amount of hours I spend outside of school doing school work. I spend about 25 hours extra completing school work when I am not at work.
-Texas Elementary school teacher, 2019

"I'm in the midst of being burned out. I woke up this morning and honestly, I was mentally tired. I was emotionally drained. I did not want to go to work."

Mr. Warren is a spiritual person. He attributes his strength to persevere during moments of emotional drain and feelings of defeat to his faith.

"My faith motivates me. Sometimes I just have to stop and say, Thank you Lord. Just that."

Mr. Warren notes that there are times when he tries and tries and at the end of the day it's like he has not done anything right.

"But I am a professional. I know my purpose and what I need to accomplish. Every experience is preparing me for a new experience, so I pray and keep it moving," he states.

So what's next?

While no one teacher experience is identical to another, there are strategies that can be used to help decrease the occurrence of frequently negative experiences in schools. Mr. Warren offers some strategies that helped him cope with his school year.

- Set priorities
- Seek support
- Surround yourself with individuals who support your best interest
- Know your limit
- Learn to say no

It is unrealistic to think that change will happen with a 360 degree turn. It will not!

However, school administrators and district leaders can help to decrease the negative impact of teacher burnout caused by workload.

Here are some suggestions from teachers:

- Elicit input from other teachers
- Eliminate redundant paperwork

- Increase manpower
- Remember other teachers need your support
- Prioritize tasks to what's impactful NOW

"It's not an issue of wants vs. needs.
It's an issue of wants vs. *Priorities.*"

-Jamie Munson

05

BAD APPLES

"People work together when it suits them.
They are loyal when it suits them.
They love each other when it suits them.
They will *betray* each other when it suits them."

—Orell

The tears swelled up in Mrs. Sawyers' eyes. The rage burned the palms of her hands. She had reached her boiling point.

"I am sick of this!
"I am just fed up with all of this!"

It was two days before Christmas Break and it had been a tough three months for Ms. Sawyers. Bogged down by the colossal amount of paperwork, never ending meetings, and disheartened by the lack of support and cooperation from her teammates, Mrs. Sawyers' emotions and tolerance had peaked.

Entering into her 6th year of teaching, Ms. Sawyers has taught in both public school and private schools. She has had experience working with teachers in middle and high schools and experience working with fellow teachers in various capacities such as coaching, mentoring, and team lead.

But this year, her teammates were making it hard for their team to be effective and successful.

Ms. Sawyers has over 6 years of teaching experience under her belt however, unlike her fellow team members she does not have a background in education. This has proven to be a challenge for her.

The pre-winter break data was due in two days. But, each member of Ms. Sawyers' team had conjured up a reason as to why they did not have their data to share at this meeting.

Previous emails and reminders went unanswered. She had enlisted the support of her and the team's supervising administrator but that proved to be worthless.

"What else can I do?
"What else can I do?!
"What- else - can I do?" Her tone fluctuating from frustration to anger to self-defeat. It was evident that Ms. Sawyers was starting to experience a decrease in self-efficacy.

"Sometimes I feel like I just don't want to do this anymore.
"I don't want to be here anymore."

> ***Approximately 8% of teachers quit teaching due to unfavorable working conditions.***
> ***-Sutcher, Darling-Hammond, & Carver-Thomas, 2006***

The ongoing uphill battle between the team members began to brew early on in the school year, after one member of the team who was hoping to become the team lead was not blessed with that position.

A matter of a fact, that team member was not granted any of her request for grade level change or alternative position at her school site.

This made that teacher furious! She went on a verbal rampage professing her detest and displeasure.

"I don't understand why they chose Sawyers over me? I can do better than her. I have been here longer than her."

Her negative comments; put down toward Ms. Sawyers; outright loathe for certain administrators, school operation, and procedures went on nonstop.

———

"Did you hear?
"Did you hear what she said?" asked a fellow colleague of Ms. Sawyers.

The bitterness of one of their team member had taken on a completely different shape when the gossip started to spread.

"Did I hear what?"
"What are you talking about?" questioned another teacher.

Early that morning the disgruntled team member began a series of conversation to voice the injustice that she felt she was dished. This spread like wildfire.

To make matters worse, she did not hold back in voicing to other coworkers via text messages of the incompetency of the teammates she was stuck with.

Research shows that teachers who were less likely to receive support from fellow teachers, were more prone to symptoms of burnout. Such as emotional exhaustion, and depersonalization.
-Pas, Bradshaw, and Hershfeldt, 2012
-Rogala, Shoji, Luszczynska, Kuna, Yeager, Benight, & Cieslak, 2016.

"I have never worked with such unsupportive and disrespectful group of people before," Ms. Sawyers mumbled as she shook her head with disbelief.

Recalling what happened during that time was still fresh like an open wound.

"From then on everything I suggested, everything I asked to get assistance with was refuted with 'Why?' 'What's the point?' 'That's not important,' 'Why do we need to do this?' 'I think this person or that person should do it.'"

The back and forth between the members of Ms. Sawyers' team got worse. Communication broke down, participation broke down. "It was everyone for themselves.

"What's the point of having a team if all we do is bicker, argue, and fuss?"

> **"We are not a team because we work together. We are a team because we respect, trust, and care for each other."**
> -Tom Wiley

But there was no respect, trust, care, or productivity with this team, among these group of teachers.

———————

"So what's the plan for today? Are we going to move forward with analyzing the data or not?"

The room stood silent. No one responded or even acknowledged the question with a nonverbal response.

The clicking sound of fingers dabbling away at the keys on the computers made it evident that their priorities were otherwise placed.

"Well," Jane said with a quiet and timid voice.
"We have been arguing about how to move forward with determining who will reteach what standard and how we will distribute these students. I think we should start from there."

"What do you mean we have been arguing about this? I have *not* been arguing about anything. Maybe you all, but not me."

"Here we go again," another team member chimed in. "There is no point being here or doing this if we are going continue arguing about the small stuff."

"Ok, ok. Let's just stop for a second. All I am saying is for us to start with discussing the standards that they scored low on, on the last assessment, then from there, just assigning students to teachers. This can be done," Ms. Sawyers stated with a firm voice.

In an environment where there is disorganization and chaos, it is important to stand out and stand firm focusing on what's the priority: students' success.

When there is a lack of colleague

support, students' success is impacted.

When surveyed, more than half of the number of teachers responded unfavorably when they did not received support from their colleagues
-Dacres, 2019.

Such negative interaction has shown to lead to teachers becoming burned out resulting in students being negatively impacted.
-Irvin, Hume, Boyd, McBee, & Odom, 2013

A fellow colleague of Ms. Sawyer's, Paul, got wind of what was going on and spoke up.

Paul had worked closely with Ms. Sawyer, but prior to that moment had no idea about what was really going on until she began to share with him. He could not believe what he was hearing from Ms. Sawyer about her team. Paul decided to do something about it. He met with his immediate supervisor who was also Ms. Sawyer's supervisor to share what was happening.

"Something needs to be done about Ms. Sawyers' team," said Paul, upon meeting with his supervisor.
"What do you mean?" the supervisor questioned.

"Well, they are about to kill each other. It's horrible. It's really bad. I mean, nothing is getting done. They are all doing their own thing, making their own test, they are not collaborating with each other, most of the time they don't even see each other," Paul expressed.

"Wait, what do you mean? I'm confused, so when they meet for their weekly meetings what do they do?" The supervisor asked.

Paul began to explain how the meetings were conducted when Ms. Sawyer's team actually met. "Well, they argue or just do their own thing. Now they are fussing about the data report that is due in two days before we leave for Winter Break." Paul stated.

"It's not done! Exclaimed the supervisor. "No," Paul replied. "Ms. Sawyers' told me that for the past two weeks it's a new excuse as to why the report is not completed," Paul added.

"Did you talk to Ms. Sawyers?" The supervisor asked.

"Yes," Paul replied

"What did she say?" the supervisor added.

With a long deep sigh, Paul responded,

"No one is contributing to the team tasks, they are being defiant and just want to do their own thing."

Paul proceeded to ask his supervisor, "How often do you attend their meetings?"

"As much as I can, well, twice per month," the supervisor replied in an uncertain tone. "But none of this was brought to my attention by anyone on the team," The supervisor added.

"So do you plan on addressing this?" Paul asked.

"Well," said Paul's supervisor, "I think I need to have a meeting with the team and then go from there."

Support from administrators can play a central role in resolving conflicts among

colleagues. Which can intern combat teacher turnover.
-Learning Policy Institute, 2017.

Ms. Sawyers and her team were the only group that did not submit their report.

The impact of such action not only affected each individual on the team, but most importantly, it affected the students that they committed to teach.

We cannot always influence or control what others do. As individuals and as leaders we aim to make a difference, to unite to achieve a goal. Our goal and our priority *must* be to ensure the academic success of all students.

"While conflict is inevitable when it comes to change, it is not the goal

> of the group to avoid it, but to learn how to manage it productively. Doing so can lead to creativity and cohesiveness.
> However, it is important to also note that repeated conflict can drain a group's energy and time."
> – DuFour, DuFour, Eaker, Many, Mattos, 2016

Working together on a team can prove to be difficult. Without an agreed upon purpose, focus, guide, and cohesiveness, the effective functioning of a team can be disrupted and be destructive. The dispute, lack of cohesiveness, and misguided priority of the teachers on Ms. Sawyers' team negatively affected their students' success.

So what's next?

Working with others can be rewarding, but it can also be difficult. Difficult people are the roadblocks between success and failure.

What do you do when you are faced with difficult people?

What can you do when they constantly work to block your progress?

What should you do to prevail?

- Don't be reactive
- Seek outside, unbiased support
- Have a one on one conversation to address the issue
- Speak to a supervisor
- Explore a change of environment or group
- Know your trigger and don't let it get to you

"The greater the loyalty of a group toward the group, the greater is the motivation among the members to achieve the goals of the group, and

the greater the probability that the group will achieve its goals."
-Rensis Likert

So where do we go from here?

While change will not come instantly, school administrators have a role in influencing teacher interaction and support.

Here are some suggestions from the teachers:
- Create a positive working environment
- Encourage teamwork
- Promote teacher collaboration
- Be proactive to defuse negative issues
- Be respectful in your communication and actions

"Keeping together is progress. Working *together* is success."
-Henry Ford.

06

I WILL KILL YOUR BABY

About 50% of teachers working in Title I schools leave the profession. The shortage is even more critical among teachers working in Special Education.

-Carver-Thomas & Darling-Hammond, 2017

The words spewed out of her mouth like a knife piercing the heart, sharp and right on target.

"I will stab you in your gut and kill your baby, you hear me?" She whispered.

Her fist curled tightly around a sharpened pencil, teeth clenched, eyes squinted, faced cringed, I could see the rage in her eyes and I knew that she could, given the opportunity she possibly would do just that.

Kenisha's action and anger did not come as a surprise to Ms. Jeter. She has often encountered harsh words, erratic behaviors, and from time to time drastic classroom disruptions.

Kenisha's behaviors would feud back and forth arguments between her and her classmates. The arguments would become so heated that instruction would stop.

"I remember that day. As usual, I greeted Kenisha and her fellow classmates at the door. I could feel it. I just knew that something was off. Something was off with her."

"Good morning Kenisha," I said in a chirpy and upbeat voice.

She just stood there, she stared at me then into the classroom, then back at me. Ms. Jeter recounted.

"I was a bit puzzled."

"Good morning," I repeated, with a smiling face.

Ms. Jeter said without warning, Kenisha pushed passed her, sending her backwards into the classroom, stepped inside, walked over to a fellow classmate and with a tight fist, hit her on the head and started pulling her hair.

"It was... It was just, I was stunned!"

Ms. Jeter was able to separate Kenisha from the other student who was visibly traumatized from the incident.

The dean was notified immediately and showed up with the SRO in less than a minute.

Ms. Jeter discussed that Kenisha's erratic behavior was not unusual. Often times she was able to intercede and deescalate most situations.

Ms. Jeter, a 4th year teacher working in a title I school has seen quite a few negative behaviors since starting in this field. Actually, her experiences have mostly been in Title I schools in low socioeconomic communities.

After graduating with her bachelor's degree, Ms. Jeter's first option was not to work with children. Actually, she made all attempts to stay clear of this field. She had other goals and aspirations, which she embarked on. However, a life-changing event propelled her into the education field.

> **A recent national survey found that less than 5% of teachers in the field intended to become teachers. The lowest reported in 45 years.**
> **- National Education Association, 2019**

Most of Ms. Jeter's classes were filled with students who had Exceptional Student Education and 504 labels. She is used to working with this population of students and actually felt comfortable and at home when working with students with learning disabilities.

However, this school year, Ms. Jeter was afforded a teacher assistant, however, that person provided support in all of her classes except Kenisha's class.

During her 4 years teaching at this school, Ms. Jeter noted seeing some of the worst behaviors she thought was possible. None of which she would have been privy to as she was not an education major.

"But my mentor and my fellow colleagues were so supportive. Honestly, I don't know how I would have survived the initial 3 years without them."

Ms. Jeter was able to form a bond with a few other teachers. Some were veteran teachers and others were within their first 3 years of teaching.

"I would go home sometimes and cry. I would even call out the next day because I was up to my eyeballs with some of the student behaviors and work to be done. I was just overwhelmed. Literally, burned out. The students' behaviors were burning me out."

Several students have shown a direct connection between teacher burnout and negative student behaviors in the classroom. Students' disrespect and verbal as well as physical aggression contribute to teacher burnout.
-Hastings & Bham, 2003.

Kenisha's action and anger did not come as a surprise.

"But those 14 words, took me by

surprise."

A few prior incidents took place with Kenisha or with Kenisha and fellow students or other teachers.

Each of these incidents were mentioned and discussed with her parent, the principal, teachers, counselors, and the staffing specialists.

Once it was identified that the behaviors were escalating, as a team, the staffing specialist and the Kenisha's guidance counselor began working with her teachers to start gathering data. This, would provide insight on her behaviors and any factors that may be triggering such behaviors.

"I must say, I work with a great team and a supportive staff."

Ms. Jeter recalled about 3 months ago

an incident with Kenisha.

"It was the last 3 minutes of class. I was using my phone as a timer. I placed the phone close to the board and left it there as I worked with other students. Shortly after the bell rung, I realized that the phone was missing."

Ms. Jeter recalled frantically calling the front office and reporting the phone missing, contacting her phone company to suspend the service and to begin tracking the phone.

"Then as I stood at the door welcoming students into my class the last period of the day, two students came up to me and said they knew who took my phone."

The students reported that Kenisha took the phone, dismantled it and threw the case in the garbage bin.

"The students said that they saw the

phone which had my picture with my family on it. I immediately called the front office and informed them of what I was told."

It was a few minutes before the bell rang for dismissal when the school resource officer brought the phone back to Ms. Jeter.

"The phone screen was broken, a chip on one of the edges. But I was just thankful to have my phone back."

Because the phone is valued over a certain amount, the school resource officer informed Ms. Jeter that she could file charges.
"I know I could file charges, but what would that accomplish? Kenisha needed help. Filing charges would not necessarily get her the help she needed."

The next day Ms. Jeter spoke with the

principal and made him aware of the most recent issue with Kenisha and her concerns for Kenisha.

"He was very supportive and immediately got the ball rolling on how to proceed."

Mr. Wyzochoshi was a first year principal in the school district. He was very strict.

"I must say, I appreciated his strictness. He was all about students' success. No matter what he had to purchase or have donated, he strongly believed in doing what it takes to ensure students were successful."

In the past Ms. Jeter was able to deescalate some of the behavioral issues with Kenisha as well as with other students.

"But I now knew things had gone too far. My baby's safety, my safety was at stake."

"Kenisha stood about 15 feet from me. She was just a small petite little girl that I had grown fund of."

When Kenisha was not in class with Ms. Jeter for 4th period math, she would sometimes report to her class as an alternative placement for other classes.

"I'm not going to turn her away. Of course not. So I had her sit in the back and complete the work for the other classes."

But on that day, Kenisha's statement was a deal breaker.

"I will stab you in your gut and kill your baby, you hear me?" she whispered. Surprised by her statement, Ms. Jeter stood still, unmovable.

"What did she just say?" I thought to myself.

Ms. Jeter descriptively recalled Kenisha's physical appearance that day as she stood in front of her. With fist clenched tightly around a sharpened pencil. Ms. Jeter described how evil Kenisha looked.

"…teeth clenched, eyes squinted, faced cringed, I could see the rage in her eyes and I knew that she could, given the opportunity she possibly would do just that."

Ms. Jeter cautiously walked over to her desk, picked up the phone and called the front office to have an administrator report to her room immediately.

"Kenisha, did not move at all. She just

stood there."

When the dean showed up, Ms. Jeter was visibly shaken up. Kenisha just stood there with her head down.

Ms. Jeter explained to the dean what happened and that she did not feel safe.
"I fear for my baby's safety." Ms. Jeter whispered, as the tears welled up in her eyes

"Kenisha, come with me," the dean said in an instructive voice.

Kenisha did not move.

"Kenisha, come with me," he repeated now with a stern voice.

The dean walked over and carefully guided Kenisha outside the classroom.

"I felt horrible, I felt like I had

failed her."

Ms. Jeter obviously wanted the best for Kenisha and although Kenisha has had numerous violent and non-violent behavior towards teachers and her peers, she knew that she could not remedy this situation. Things were now out of her hands.

The next day, Ms. Jeter was informed that Kenisha would no longer be in her class and that she was suspended for making a threat to a teacher.
Kenisha never returned to school.

"Every once in a while I think about her. Where she is now? What may have happened to her? Sometimes, I think what else I could have done. Does she blame me for any negative repercussions that may have happened due to her actions that day?"

As Ms. Jeter recalled her experiences working in a Title I school, she was brought to the awareness that throughout those years and experiences she had also experienced symptoms of burnout.

Leaving work exhausted after a day of daunting tasks and stress from students. Disrespect and threats from students. Sleepless nights, crying spells, and not wanting to return to work the next day.

"I was frequently fatigued, stressed, frustrated as to why teaching was like this. It shouldn't be."

At the time Ms. Jeter had no idea that she was in the midst of being burned out.

"I tell you, knowledge is power. I am now aware of the triggers and symptoms of burnout. I will never go back to that place!"

Teacher turnover is 50% higher in Title I schools compared to other types of school.

Math and Science teachers leave the field at a rate of 70% higher in Title I schools.

Moreover, teachers with alternative certification working in Title I schools are 80% more likely to leave the classroom.
-Carver-Thomas & Darling-Hammond, 2017.

These alarming numbers are due to the many negative factors affecting these group of teachers such as students' negative behaviors, excessive workload, and the lack of support in the working environment, leading to burnout.

So, what's next?

Addressing teacher burnout is critical to the teacher attrition crisis. So what can be done now to help alleviate this crisis?

Here are some suggestions that teachers have proposed:
- Allow for teacher autonomy
- Provide adequate administrator support
- Allow for meaningful and adequate time to collaborate with colleagues
- Support teachers experiencing negative student behaviors
- Promote a cohesive and safe working environment

"When you are stuck in the burnout abyss. When you feel like all hope is lost. Don't be dismayed, just remember too much is at stake to bow out now. You are making a difference in the life of a child."

-Sherika Dacres

07

DON'T CHANGE HORSES MIDSTREAM ... OR SHOULD YOU?

"Success is not final.
Failure is not fatal.
It is the *courage* to continue that counts."

-John Wooden

"They say, you never know what you have until it's gone. My realization of the value of what I had, came a little too late."

As a seasoned teacher of 18 years, Shonda knew from the time she was a young girl that she was destined to become a teacher.

As a child, she would often play school teacher with her younger siblings and her neighbors, and yes, she was always the teacher.

"I used to remember what it was like for me when I was in my own class and then go home and relive that same experience, and I was the teacher. It felt good. They were listening to me and I was telling them what to do."

Yes, for Shonda, initially, it was all about telling others what to do. But the realization of the blessing and curse of being a teacher came later on.

Shonda grew up in a middle class neighborhood in an urban community. Most young women in her community selected one of three options: becoming a nurse, a teacher, or getting married and becoming a housewife. For Shonda, option three was not an option right now. She was terrified of blood and sick people, so option one was out. But being a teacher was a passion that she had always carried within.

> **The desires of a man's heart is knowing who he is and what he wants, and following his dreams to get there.**
> **-Unknown**

Shonda went away to college, shortly after her high school graduation. "There was no time for a break," Shonda recalled. "I just felt that I had a lot to accomplish and spending time in college partying and chilling was just not on my radar."

Taking no time off, spearing no time to relax and enjoy life as a young college girl, Shonda was able to complete her bachelor's degree in less than two years and graduate shortly after with her master's degree.

Her senior externship opened the door for what she thought was "the dream job."

"I have always wanted to work with children in a low socio-economic environment. I just felt that I could do so much more and that my experience and what I had to offer would be more appreciated," Shonda explained.

Shonda started out as a 7th grade Science teacher. However, she later found out that her teaching assignment was changed.

"I received a call from the assistant principal the Friday before pre-planning week. First she wanted to verify my certifications and wanted to know if I had my English Speakers of Other Languages (ESOL) certification, which I did."

Shonda said the assistant principal continued the conversation by expressing how impressed she was with her during the interview and how happy they are that she is now a part of the family.

Shonda continued, "Then the assistant principal said, unfortunately, due to our student count and needs, we will need to move you out of the Science class and into an ESOL class."

"ESOL class?" I thought to myself. "I knew what ESOL was; I had an idea of what is an ESOL class, but, ESOL class? What did that mean for me?

"Okay." I replied.
"What does that mean?" I asked.
"Well, that means you will have 6 classes in which most, if not all, of the students will be bilingual. But, you have your certification and I trust that you were able to get some training during your college courses." The assistant principal replied.

Shonda was taken aback by what she just heard from the assistant principal.

"I was shocked! Lost for words. Not okay," Shonda thought to herself.
"No, I don't agree, I don't understand."

But those were just thoughts, not Shonda's reply. The words out of Shonda's mouth were a variety of "Okay, I understand, ok." That was all Shonda could muster up to say.

"I don't really remember taking a lot of courses that focused on working with ESOL students. Well, I do, but not really. What we may have done was to complete various activities and scenarios that included ELL/ESOL students, but I don't recall being placed in a class for my internship where I was exposed to or worked consistently with these individuals."

Research shows that the number of ELL/ESOL students in U.S classrooms are growing rapidly.

In 2015 close to 10% of ESOL/ELL students were registered in K-12 public schools, a 2% jump from 2010.

-National Center for Education Statistics, 2019

Meanwhile, as the number of students enrolled in ELL/ESOL increases, teachers are still unprepared to work with these learners.

A week before the start of the new school year, Shonda was able to meet with a group of teachers with whom she was expected to work closely with. Over the next few days Shonda worked independently as well as collaboratively with her peers to prepare for the quarterly lessons.

"I felt a bit confused, actually, very confused at times. While I knew what I was supposed to do, I was lost on how I would best work with and support these students."

Less than 13% of the approximately 40% of public school teachers working with ESOL/ELL students, have the proper training to support ELL/ESOL students.
-Quintero & Hansen, 2017

Shonda recalled talking with a group of teachers, some of whom had been teaching for several years, others were within their first 5 years of teaching. "So," Shonda begun. "I was told that I am now teaching 5 periods of ESOL classes, and 1 period as a support teacher. Does that mean I will have all the bilingual students?"

"Yes," one of her colleagues replied.

"Are you sure that's your teaching assignment?" another questioned.

"As of Friday, yes," Shonda replied.

Oftentimes teachers are hired for one position, but are reassigned to another position or role, or will have to take on additional duties based on the school's needs. Most teachers do not question or oppose such decisions.

> **Teacher shortage topped over 100,000 in the 2017/2018 school year, and the numbers do not appear to be going down.**
> **-Sutcher, Darling-Hammond, & Carver-Thomas, 2016**

A 2016 poll found that schools across the nation were starting and students were sitting in class without an assigned teacher to start the school year. Well, what does that mean for students? The lack of qualified teachers threatens the effective learning of students. It affects the ability of an equitable education for all.

What does that mean for teachers? They will have to take on more than what they bargained for. The burden may now fall on them to take on more classes and additional duties to offset this deficit.

―――――――

The first week of school begun and

Shonda felt as prepared as she could be. Her classes were no more than 16 students. She had her lessons mapped out and felt confident with what she had to teach. However, her struggles soon begun.

After the fourth week of school, Shonda realized that most of her students were still not mastering the lesson she taught.

"I know what I was teaching was accurate, but I just felt out of my skin. Well, I did not feel that I was reaching my students."

"Well I don't have any support to help model for me

what to do with these students, so I can't help them."

-Report from a Reading Teacher, In Samuels, 2017

"I let them sit in the back because I don't know what else to do with them."

-Report from a ELA Teacher, In Samuels, 2017

Shonda stated that she enlisted the help of a fellow colleague, however, the support was minimal as each individual on her team had their own battles they were fighting.

"I began to feel alone." Shonda recalled.

"I was new to teaching, new to working with ESOL students, and the support system, well, that was none existent. I felt defeated."

Shonda's decreased feeling in her ability to complete task or job duties effectively is one of the dimension of burnout, known as reduced personal accomplishment. This feeling is brought on when an individual no longer feels that what he or she is doing is effective. A person questions his or her competency to complete job duties.

"When I first started my career as a teacher 19 years ago, I was thrown into it. I was like a dog to the slaughter. For real. No experience, no explicit guide, it was just, here you go. All the best. That was it. How did I cope you are probably wondering. Well, I faked it. Honestly, once I got in front of those children, I just faked it. I acted like I was teaching for years. And when any of them asked, I would say, I've been doing this for quite some time. That was it. When someone came in to observe me, I would reteach a lesson from before, I would bribe my students with candy or no homework for a week. Just anything to ensure that I did not look like a newbie, or like I did not know what I was doing. But, that only lasted for a while. Soon, I had to know what I was doing. The candy ran out. My students became bored. I just had to get on my 'A' game. So, I sought out individuals who I knew were teaching for a while. And wow, they had all the good stuff. Some things I did not agree with, they were just older ways of teaching which contradicted what I learned in college. But others were golden advice. I took what I could use and applied it. I began to read more about the students I was working with. I signed up for trainings and professional developments. These saved me. Saved me mentally, emotionally, physically. Saved my career. Now I'm almost 20 years in. Looking back asking for help and seeking support was all worth it."

-Assistant Principal Ruth

Shonda's experience is not uncommon. Forced into a role with which one does not have the experience or competence to work in is not new to the education system. Likewise, not having the support needed on hand is also not new to the field of education.

"I remembered we were a few weeks from Winter Break. Just around the time to wrap up the second quarter. I spent several hours after work on campus, and the coffee shop and at home to complete my lesson plans. I was able to research information online that provided additional insight to work with ESOL students."

Shonda expressed her unhappiness with

not being able to attend many district professional development meetings or trainings because this would require that she used her own personal or sick time.

"But when my team was able to meet one-on-one or as a group, I would plan with them and get suggestions on how to incorporate various strategies to increase student comprehension. I finally began to feel comfortable and confident in what I was doing."

Shonda completed the final lesson before the quarter ended. At the end of the lesson, she gave a 3 question formative assessment. She would use this information to gauge students' comprehension and plan for the upcoming lesson and any re-teaching activity.

"I sat at my desk during lunch and began reviewing their responses. I looked through the first five responses. At first, I thought I might have mixed up the questions. There was no way everyone so far got all their responses wrong. As I kept going, more and more I realized that most were getting two of the three questions wrong."

If a teacher has taught a lesson once or twice, at what point does he or she reflect and assess his or her own teaching method to determine if the error is with the student or the teacher?

> **"Self-reflection can be a valuable tool that helps make make you aware of how you are teaching, which in turn makes you a better teacher."**
>
> **-Administrate.com, 2019**

"I did not feel that working with ESOL students was the right fit for me."

Shonda blames the lack of academic training and internship exposure with this population as the cause of her lack of competency, decreased personal accomplishment, and decreased self-efficacy as the culprits for her struggles with working with this population. Additionally, while there was some colleague support, there was limited administrator support.

Shonda believed that if she had taken more specific courses and had some direct experiences working with ESOL students, she would have been better prepared.

Shonda's struggles lasted through the end of the school year.

"My biggest regret was not being more proactive and persistent with getting support. But I just had no clue it would have been this difficult."

"Failure is not fatal.
It is the courage to
continue that counts."
-John Wooden

So what's next?

School districts have a duty to their teachers and students.

Teacher training programs have a duty to the teachers who will be working with diverse group of students and to the students themselves.

Not providing teachers with the appropriate and effective teacher trainings and exposure to learning environments that will allow teachers to effectively and efficiently work with diverse students to promote learning for all is an injustice to all students.

So what can be done to remedy the issue of teachers' lack of preparedness to work with all students?

Here are some suggestions:
- School districts can provide frequent and accessible professional developments, and trainings, observations for working with ESOL students
- School districts can ensure that teacher preparedness programs are offering specific courses

focusing on working with ESOL students
- School districts can work with teacher preparedness programs to ensure that new teachers have firsthand internship experience working with ESOL students

"Although it may push our buttons and challenge us to move outside our comfort zones, we should consider small changes that can make a difference."
-Alexis Wiggins

08

WEATHERING THE BURN

"*Self-care* is not selfish. You cannot *serve* from an empty vessel."

-Eleanor Brown

"**B**eing selfish saved me from a state of emotional insanity."

They say one cannot take care of others until he or she takes care of oneself.

Mr. Hue began to rummage through the pile of papers stacked on his desk. But it was time for him to leave.

It was time to just pack up and go home, Mr. Hue thought to himself.

But he couldn't seem to tear himself away from all the work that stood motionless on his desk.

Mr. Hue is a 7-year Special Education teacher. After completing his Masters of Education degree, he landed a job at an inner city school as a Special Education teacher.

He immediately fell in love with the children. He loved his job.

"It was like I had final found my purpose... my calling. The reason why I had chosen to become a teacher," Mr. Hue expressed.

The spark in his eyes and the smile on his face was a genuine indicator of Mr. Hue's passion and love for teaching. He detail his years of teaching and working with Special Education students, his facial expression and body language jerked back and forth between each story. It was visible through each of the stories that with each joyous experience, there were some that took a toll on him. These stories appear to take Mr. Hue back to a place of discomfort and appreciation all at the same time.

After 5 years of traveling 2 hours round trip to and from work, staying late at work, and getting home after his children had fallen asleep, Mr. Hue changed schools to be closer to home. The change was needed!

In no time Mr. Hue settled in at his new school and began to develop relationships that proved to be experience and how instrumental his self-care and survival was for him as an educator.

———

Over the past few years Mr. Hue has noticed a sharp rise in the amount of work tasks he has had to contend with. But, through it all, he continued to prevail, often reflecting on the joy and contentment he found working as a Special Education teacher.

———

"After this I will leave," Mr. Hue muttered to himself, trying desperately to convince himself that the time he was sacrificing from his family was worth it.

"I'm almost finished," he thought, trying hard not to glance at the clock on the wall.

Before you know it, Mr. Hue is rushing to his car to avoid getting locked inside the school compound.

"Surely this could not be healthy," Mr. Hue thought to himself as he drove down the long stretch of road leading to his home.

Like him, hundreds of other teachers also travel the same path and experience some of the same ills of being an educator. Being overwhelmed, overworked, exhausted, frustrated, sometimes withdrawn, and disconnected. But, the love for being a teacher, the love for wanting to make a difference in a child's life, often outweighs these ills.

Many compelling arguments have been put forward as to why the issue of teacher burnout *must* be addressed and resolved.

Heart attack!

High blood pressure!

Stroke!

Research has shown there is a direct connection between experiences of burnout and physical illnesses. These ailments can

incapacitate teachers.
-Saboori and Pishghadam,
2016; U.S. Department of
Health and Human Services,
DHHS, 2019

Mr. Hue, recalls about three years into his career that he started to feel uncomfortable emotionally and physically. At that time, not thinking much of it, he brushed it off, But the ongoing feelings of begin emotionally depleted persisted. His workdays continued to be long, his workload increased, his responsibilities doubled. He was burdened, exhausted, devoured by the day-to-day stressful factors complementary of his job.

He recalled an incident with his daughter not too long ago.

"I remember one night when I arrived home late and quietly tried to open the garage door, my daughter met me at the door. 'Dad,' she said. 'I can't fall asleep.' I asked, why, but, I kinda knew the answer."

Mr. Hue, wanted to hear his daughter say it. He thought, maybe if his daughter said the words, voiced how worried she was that her father was coming home late at night; How she felt like her father was not there when she needed him, her fear of not having her father around, maybe, just maybe, Mr.

Hue would have no choice but to face reality. To face the fact that he had been putting his job before his own well-being and his family.

> **Before I can help other people. I need to take care of my own inner demons. I need to make sure that I am in a good mental state. Only THEN, once I am in a good place, should I try to help others.**
> **-Troy Erstling, 2017**

The next morning Mr. Hue met up with his closest coworkers. He put everything on the table and confided in them, sharing how overwhelmed and exhausted he had become. The more he shared, the more he wanted to share. It was like an onion and with each layer that was peeled off, the less the weight of the burden he felt. His colleagues were in disbelief. How could they have not noticed this? They thought all along he had it all figured out.

"Wow, really?" one of the three colleagues responded. "We knew you had a lot on your plate, but we had no idea that it was taking such a toll on you," she added.

"What can we do to help? You know we are here for you," another chimed in.

"I don't want you to go through this alone. You know we are here for you."

Mr. Hue knew the support he had from his coworkers. He knew that they would step in and help out however they could.

Collegial support and collaboration between teachers decreases teacher's negative perception of the work environment. The lack of such support could lead to teacher burnout.
Dacres, 2019; Skaalvik & Skaalvik, 2016

Mr. Hue soon found out that he was not the only one experiencing feelings of exhaustion and being overwhelmed. His colleagues each shared how they too experienced firsthand some of the ills of being a teacher. While they too loved their work as a teacher, they also shared how the increased demands of work had, at times, made them want to quit.

One of his colleagues recalled his experience of being burned out about 4 years ago.

"I honestly became angry, angry at work, angry at my colleagues, I kind of resented my job," Mr. Hue's colleague expressed. "I woke up some mornings and did not even want to go to work. I came into work and was mentally not there, I felt that what I was doing was just not cutting it. But, my mentor at that time literally helped save me, saved my career. She shared with me some of the things I was doing that was physically and mentally killing me. For example, taking work home, working nonstop on the weekends, staying at work late. I just could not seem to stop. But with her support, I did. I prioritized and made a change. I had to change what I was doing for the sake of my health, my sanity."

93% of teachers blamed their workload as a direct factor in their decision to leave teaching.

-National Education Union, 2018

Mr. Hue's colleague pointed out how they were all suffering in some shape or form working as a teacher. Suffering because of the career they chose. Suffering for the children they vowed to work with.

However, they have found that if they rally around each other and support one another, they can decrease the symptoms and experiences of burnout.

"I have since realized how important it is as a teacher to clothe myself with individuals around me that can help me mentally and physically cope with the highs and lows of being a teacher," Mr. Hue concluded.

> **What breaks you down is not the amount of pressure you feel at one time, but it's the way you perceive and handle it.**
> **-Lena Horne**

So what's next?

Increased teacher workload is causing

increased feelings of stress and emotional exhaustion, and this is driving teachers away.

It is essential that additional light is shed upon the excessive amount of work that teachers continues to face in the work environment. Some teachers work upwards of 50 hours per week in an effort to keep up with their increasingly high work demands.

Flanked by the enormous amount of paperwork and other job duties to perform, and the guilt of feeling less than enough when students do not show academic success, teachers bear the constant burden of feeling emotionally exhausted and overwhelmed.

So what can be done to begin to bring resolution to the issue of the teachers work overload?

Here are some suggestions:

- Administrators should continue to intentionally provide teachers with the opportunity to have meaningful work collaborations
- Administrators should conduct ongoing assessments of teachers' workload and job duties, and actively work with teachers to create a plan of action to remedy teacher work overload
- School district leaders should work with schools and teachers

to develop effective strategies to cope with and decrease teacher workload

- School leaders and school district leaders should provide frequent and accessible professional developments and trainings targeting work-life/workload management
- School districts and school leaders can work with new teachers to provide access to colleague support and effective coping strategies for workload and work-life management

"The most valuable resources that all teachers have is each other. Without *collaboration*, our growth is limited to our own perspectives"

- Robert John Meehan

EPILOGUE

Like many other professions, and at the same time unlike many other professions, the field of education can be rewarding, yet deadly. So many teachers have entered this profession with great intentions, only to soon leave feeling burned out and defeated. The impact of being burned out has left teachers feeling emotionally depleted, and physically and mentally drained.

An estimated 50% of current classroom teachers will leave the profession within the next 5 years. If this is not shocking enough, nearly 20% of new teachers and close to 50% of urban teachers who enter the classroom are projected to leave within three to five years.

But why?

Teacher burnout is not a new phenomenon, but it continues to disrupt and impinge on the lives of educators. The plight of burnout experienced by K-12 teachers remains unbearable with no signs of remedy in the near future. Teachers are suffering from the insurmountable workload, lack of support, students' negative behaviors, and decreased feelings of self-efficacy experienced in their work environment.

While the mental, emotional, and physical scars of burnout are not worn on their sleeves, nor tattooed on their foreheads, the salient effects of teacher burnout are evident through their stories shared.

This book gave you a bird's eye view of some of the factors contributing to the lived experiences of teachers who have succumb to the ills of burnout.

Likewise, it is a call to action to push to the forefront discussions of the impact of teacher burnout on educators, students, and the education system on a whole.

It is my hope that the stories shared in this book will inspire more intentional conversations about teacher burnout among teachers, administrators, school district leaders, mental health professionals, and other stakeholders alike. Through such conversations, I hope that solutions will be birthed that will work toward decreasing teacher burnout and in turn decrease the attrition rate among teachers so as to effect ongoing student academic growth success.

GLOSSARY

Burnout: Prolonged exposure to ongoing stressors in the work environment leading to increased emotional exhaustion, increased feelings of detachment from the job, and decreased feelings of accomplishment.

Depersonalization: When a person becomes negative and detached from others.

Emotional Exhaustion: Feelings of tension and being overwhelmed brought on by school overload or increased school demands.

Personal Accomplishment: Feelings of low morale and belief in one's self to perform job tasks.

Professional Learning Committee (PLC): A group of educators who meet to collaborate and share ideas and expertise to improve their individual teaching skills and students' academic performance.

Self-Efficacy: The belief in oneself that he or she is able to complete a given task and achieve ones goals.

Teacher: A person who helps other individuals acquire knowledge and to perform specific tasks.

Workload: The amount of work and complexity required to complete a task in a given time.

REFERENCES AND FURTHER READINGS

Aldrup, K., Klusmann, U., Ludtke, O., Gollner, R., & Trautwein, U.
(2018). *Learning and Instruction, 58*, 126-136.
https://doi.org/10.1016/j.learninstruc.2018.05.006

Anthony, J. (2019). 7 conclusions from the worlds largest teacher survey. Retrieved from:
https://notwaitingforsuperman.org/teacher-burnout-statistics/

Bandura, A. (2010). Self-Efficacy. *The Corsini Encyclopedia of Psychology.* https://doi.org/10.1002/9780470479216.corpsy0836

Carver-Thomas & Darling-Hammond, L. (2017). Teacher Turnover: Why it matters and what we can do about it. Learning Policy Institute. Retrieved from: https://learningpolicyinstitute.org/product/teacher-turnover-report

CEA, 2018. Rise in aggressive behaviors in the classroom impacting students, teachers. Retrieved from: http://www.cea.org/issues/press/2018/mar/14/rise-in-aggressive-student-behavior-in-the-classroom-impacting-students-teachers.cfm

Diaz, C. I. (2018). The truth about teacher burnout: It's work induced depression. *American Psychological Association*. Retrieved from: http://psychlearningcurve.org/the-truth-about-teacher-burnout/

Hastings, R.P and Bham, M.S. (2003). The relationship between student behavior patterns and teacher burnout. *School Psychology International, 24*(1), 115-127

Hinds, D. (2019). Teachers say workload is driving them out of the profession. Retrieved from: https://news.sky.com/story/40-of-teachers-to-leave-role-by-2024-over-workload-and-accountability-survey-says-11695351#:~:text=While%2040%25%20of%20educators%20polled,not%20conducive%20to%20family%20life.%22

Ingersoll, R. & Perda, D. (2012). How high is teacher turnover and is it a problem? Philadelphia: Consortium for Policy in Research in Education, University of Pennsylvania.

Lawrence, D.F., Loi, N.M., & Gudex, B. W. (2019). Understanding the relationship between work intensification and burnout in secondary teachers, *Teachers and Teaching, 25*(2), 189-199, DOI: 10.1080/13540602.2018.1544551

Learning Policy Institute. (2017). *The Role of Principals in Addressing Teacher Shortages* (research brief). Palo Alto, CA: Learning Policy Institute

Long, C. (2012). Bullying of teachers pervasive in many schools. National Education Association. Retrieved from: http://neatoday.org/2012/05/16/bullying-of-teachers-pervasive-in-many-schools-2/

Maslach, C. (1982). The cost of caring. Englewood Cliffs, NJ: Prentice Hall; 1982.

Maslach, C. & Leiter, M. P. (2016). Understanding the burnout experience: Recent research and its implications for psychiatry. *World Psychiatry, 15*(2), 103-111. Doi:10.1002/wps.20311

Murray, C. (2019). How many hours do

educators really work? Retrieved from: https://edtechmagazine.com/K-12/article/2013/08/how-many-hours-do-educators-actually-work

Mrachko, A. A., Kostewicz, D. E., & Martin, W. P. (2017). Increasing positive and decreasing negative teacher responses to student behavior through training and feedback. *Behavior Analysis: Research and Practice, 17*(3), 250-265. http://dx.doi.org/10.1037/bar0000082

National Educational Association (NEA). 2019. Survey: Number of Future Teachers Reaches All-time Low. Retrievedfrom: http://neatoday.org/2016/03/15/future-teachers-at-all-time-low/

National Education Association (NEA). (2019). Research spotlight on recruiting & retaining highly qualified teachers: Recruiting &

retaining a highly qualified, diverse teaching workforce. Retrieved from: http://www.nea.org/tools/17054.htm

National Education Union (2018). Teachers' Workload. Retrieved from: https://neu.org.uk/media/3136/view

Quintero, D., & Hansen, M. (2017). English learners and the growing need for qualified teachers. Brown Center Chalkboard (blog), Brookings Institution.

National Education Association (NEA). 2018. Teacher compensation: Fact vs. Fiction. Retrieved from: www.nea.org/home/12661.htm

Strauss, V. (2019). A 'staggering' 30,000 teachers in Oklahoma have left the profession in the past 6 years.Retrievedfrom: https://www.washingtonpost.com/educati

on/2019/03/05/staggering-teachers-oklahoma-have-left-profession-last-years-heres-why/?noredirect=on&utm_term=.c6a0dc2bd1ac

Rogala, A., Shoji, K., Luszczynska, A., Kuna, A., Yeager, C., Benight, C.C., & Cieslak, R. (2016). From exhaustion to disengagement via self-efficacy change: Findings from two longitudinal studies among human services workers. *Frontier in Psychology.* Doi: 10.3389/fpsyg.2015.02032

Samuels, S. (2017). Bridging the Gap between ESOL and Native English Speakers in a Digital Collaborative Classroom. Electronic Theses and Dissertations, 2004-2019. 5519. https://stars.library.ucf.edu/etd/5519

Sutcher, L., Darling-Hammond, L., & Carver-Thomas, D. (2016). *A coming* crisis in teaching? Teacher supply, demand, and shortages in the U.S.* Palo Alto, CA: Learning Policy Institute https://learningpolicyinstitute.org/product/coming-crisis-teaching

Uliano, D. (2018). Why are so many DC teachers leaving their jobs? Retrieved from: https://wtop.com/dc/2018/10/contracts-evaluation-process-linked-to-high-dc-teacher-turnover-rates/

Weale, S. (2019). Fifth of teachers plan to leave the profession within two years: National Education Union warns of exodus caused by excessive workloads. *The Guardian.* Retrieved from: https://www.theguardian.com/education/2019/apr/16/fifth-of-teachers-plan-to-leave-profession-within-two-years

ABOUT THE AUTHOR

Dr. Sherika Simone is an Educational Psychologist, educator, and author of the book "Death by Burnout: Education's Dirty Little Secret". She has spent the last decade researching the impact of burnout on teachers working in various school types, such as traditional public schools and charter schools.

Sherika has a Ph.D. in Psychology and has more than 15 years experience working in K-12 and higher education settings.

She is a co-host of the radio program Central Florida Education Pioneers.

Sherika resides in Florida with her family.

Made in the USA
Middletown, DE
08 March 2025